THE KEY TO CAMELOT

Tintagel Peninsula

Introduction

The wind rustled the brown locks of a small boy who looked out onto the sea. Standing on the edge of the Atlantic Ocean he looked out to Tintagil castle and across to Merlins Cave. He had been brought to the site that was named in the Arthurian legends as the place of the conception of King Arthur. Tintagel, on the North Cornwall coast, was the most beautiful natural formation. A grass covered peninsular one mile in circumference, shaped like a lions paw, with a narrow crossing point it was a fortress carved by the forces of nature. It sheer grey cliffs plunged down 250 feet to the sea raging beneath. Sat at his fathers knee the tale of King Arthur unfolded in front of him,

'Long, long ago there was a King and his name was Uther Pendragon. He had a wife Igraine who was Queen of Tintagil. They had a son Arthur but the boy was given away at birth to Merlin the Magician who had him raised by an old knight, Sir Ector. When Arthur was a baby the King died and the land fell into disorder. When Arthur was a young man he was taken by Sir Ector to a joust with Ector's son Kay. When they arrived they found that a sword had been placed in an anvil on a stone in the churchyard. On the sword was written, 'whoever shall pull this sword from this stone and anvil will be rightways king born of all England'. Arthur stepped up to the sword gripped the handle and pulled it out and was hailed as the true King.

After his coronation Arthur won many battles, however his sword was broken in mortal combat with a knight named Sir Pellinore. Arthur needed a worthy replacement so one night Merlin took him to a moonlit lake and told him that the lady of the lake would bequeath him a sword Excalibur. Merlin decreed that the power of this sword would be so great that he who carried it would not be defeated in battle. Arthur took a small boat and rowed out onto the lake. When he was there an arm covered in silk came from below the water holding a sword and scabbard. Arthur reached out, grasped the pommel and the hand disappeared beneath the still surface of the lake.

Arthur married Gwynevere who had a castle at Camelot. At their wedding her father King Lodegrance gave a present of a round table to King Arthur, and all of the knights gathered around it. Arthur made Camelot his capital and he lived there with Queen Gwynevere. There was a feast and the knights were gathered at Camelot and there appeared in front of them a cup, the holy grail, covered in silk. They wished to see it but they were so mesmerised that they failed to remove the silk before the grail had disappeared. The knights vowed to go in search of the grail. It took many months and much hardship but in the end three of the knights were carried by a silk covered ship which took them to the castle of Corbenic. There they were welcomed in by the King of Corbenic, Pelles, who led them to a hall where a feast had been prepared. Whilst they were eating the holy grail was revealed to them but it's power was so strong that two of the knights were killed.

The remaining knight Sir Bors returned to Camelot. For a while the kingdom was at peace, however Gwynevere had fallen in love with Sir Lancelot, a knight of the round table. When Arthur discovered this he was forced to flee to his castle in the North, called the Joyous Castle, and Gwynevere was sentenced to death on a fire. As the flames licked around her heels Sir Lancelot returned on a white horse, plucked her from the pyre and took her away to his castle. Arthur raised an army to capture Lancelot, however whilst he was fighting him Arthur's son Mordred, seeing the opportunity to sieze the kingdom from his father, raised an army against him and the land was riven in two. The King's pursuit of Lancelot was abandoned and he returned to fight Mordred.

The two met in battle on Salisbury Plain, and the fight was fierce with brave knights being cut down on every side. In the end the battlefield was littered with corpses. As dusk began to fall King Arthur spied Sir Mordred in the distance. He rushed at him with a spear, thrusting it clean through Mordred's body, however in his death throes Mordred struck Arthur on the side of the head with his sword and he fell in a swoon. The battle was over, but Arthur was mortally wounded. He was carried through the night on horseback by two of his bravest and most loyal knights, Sir Bedevyre and Sir Lucan. They took him to the side of a lake where he gave his sword Excalibur to Sir Bedevyre who threw it into the water. As the sword flew through the air a hand covered in silk rose from beneath the surface, caught it, brandished it three times and then vanished beneath the waves.

When the sword had gone there appeared out of the mists a barge carrying nine ladies, and each one of them was a Queen. Then Sir Bedyvere took King Arthur on his back and carried him to the waters edge where the ladies took him into the barge and carried him away to the isle of Avalon to heal his wounds. Some men said that King Arthur did not die but was carried by the will of the Gods into another place, and some said that he would come again and win back his holy kingdom. All I know is that he was carried to a different world.'

As the father ended the tale the son asked

"Where is Camelot and what is the Grail?"

but the father did not know.

AVEBURY AND THE ORIGINS OF THE QUEST

This is the story of my quest to find Camelot and uncover the truth of the Grail legend. The quest was in part a search for the geographical and historical truth behind the Arthurian legends, but more importantly it was a search for it's core philosophy, elements of which have remained central to life in the modern era. Although the physical Cameot is important it is actually the ideals behind it that are key. In particular the meaning of the Grail legend is central to unlocking the value in the Arthurian legends.

The search itself started with a trip to Avebury one evening in the Winter of 1989. On the road leading to Avebury there is an enormous conical burial, over a hundred feet high in height. The site is called Silbury Hill and is the largest man-made prehistoric mound in Europe.

Silbury Hill

The main Avebury site is a mile from the mound. It consists of a large circular ridge which encloses a ditch. Within this are large stones in a circle, approximately hundred stones existed initially although many are missing, and inside this are a furthur two circles of stone with about fifty stones in total when the site was constructed. The stones are large, up to fifteen feet square and three feet in depth although many were smaller and are made of a whitish grey stone called sarsen. Outside the circle itself are two parallel rows of stones 50 feet apart leading slightly to the left of Silbury which is visible in the distance from the top of the ridge. The circle had roads crossing it both north south and east west, which cut through what appeared to be natural entrance points to the circle. A large part of the village of Avebury is inside the circlar ditch.

Avebury Stone Circle

Near to Avebury is a site called the Sanctury, which has been recently excavated.

Initial investigations of the site revealed that Avebury was many thousands of years old and from the pre Roman era. However most source material sheds little light on the original purpose of the site. Additionally they almost no information on the likely philosophy of the site builders. In order to understand Avebury it is necessary to visit Stonehenge, which provides some direct connections to the Arthurian legends.

STONEHENGE

A few weeks after the trip to Avebury I travelled to Stonehenge.

Stonehenge takes the form of a circle of stones, many fallen or leaning. Outside the circle on the eastern side is single large stone, facing towards the sunrise
The site originally consisted of a circle of 56 large stones with an average height of 13 feet. Inside that was another horseshoe of smaller stones called blue stones about four feet in height.

Stonehenge

The stone outside the circle to the east was called the heel stone, and there were four other positions outside the circle marked by smaller round 'station stones'. The stones themselves were the same colour as those at Avebury.

The original traditions were widely thought to have been lost in the mists of time. As with Avebury I have always found it hard to believe that the traditions and ideology which had been responsible for the building such a huge monument had been entirely lost. In the case of Stonehenge there is an interetsing legend that Merlin was the builder of the site, which originates from the History of the Kings of Britain, written in 1138. Merlin is a philosophical character who had many ideas which could be the key to the way of thinking of the builders of the circles. Additionally the magic nature of the circle continues to exist in modern British culture.

The Calendar of the Stonehenge Era

Stonehenge is widely associated with the Summer Solstice. The reason for this is that there is a stone which sits outside the main circle called the heel stone. On Midsummer morning the sun rising over the horizon aligns with this stone as seen from the centre of the circle. To discover the remains of the traditions of Stonehenge the calendar is a good place to start as calenders are integrally associated with the culture of a nation. If the traditions from the period of the original Stonehenge builders were still continuing then it would be expected that their remnants would be visible in the festivals of the modern year.

Stonehenge is also associated with Druidry and it is important to understand this connection to truly understand the meaning of the monument. It was clear that before Christianity came to Britain there was a calendar which had been replaced. It is critical to understand whether the pre Roman calendar had had a celebration on the summer solstice, or whether this connection was created later artificially by modern Druids.

It is widely known that the festival of Christmas replaced a festival of on the winter solstice and dated from pre Roman times. The name of the winter solstice festival was called Yule and Christ's birthday was only placed on the winter solstice around 400AD. Where Christianity came to a country which had a strongly established spiritual tradition it tended to work with it rather than take it head on in order to ease the process of conversion of the population. Thus it natural to assume that elements of the pre Christian calendar worked their way into the modern version.

The major festivals that are celebrated by everyone rather than being predominantly Christian festivals are Yule, Pancake Day, Easter, Mayday, Harvest Festival, and Guy Fawkes night. If you divide up the year into eight equal parts starting with the winter solstice you got the following dates.

21st December
5th February
21st March
5th May
21st June
5th August
21st September
5th November

When I looked at the dates of the six major festivals I noticed that they basically all fell on one of these days. The obvious one was Guy Fawkes night on 5th November. Mayday also provided a close fit. In Britain this falls on the first Monday of the month, which is always between 1st and 7th May. Additionally Harvest Festival always falls on the first Sunday after the 21st September, the Spring Equinox. Yule it seemed clear to me was based on the winter solstice. Easter falls on the Sunday following the first full moon after the Spring Equinox. In theory therefore it can fall on the 23rd March two days after the Equinox. In the same way as Christmas in linked to the Winter solstice, Easter is linked to the autumn equinox. The Concise Oxford Dictionary defines Easter as

"Easter/ n 1. (also Easter Day or Sunday) the festival (held on a variable Sunday in March or April) commemorating Christ's resurrection.....[from] Eostre, a goddess associated with spring.

showing that Christianity did indeed merge its traditions with preexistent pagan ones. This also explained the fact that pancake day did not fall on 5th February. The reason for it's move was that it had apparently been taken up by Christians to celebrate the start of Lent. Since Christianity had gone as far as adopting a pagan name for its major festival then there was a strong likelihood that other elements of the pre Christian calendar had survived.

It is widely accepted that the pre Roman traditions attached a meaning to the year in that it followed through a life cycle starting with eggs at the beginning of the year, courting at Mayday, harvest, and finally death on Guy Fawkes night, where an effigy is burnt on a bonfire. The evergreen tree is then brought into the house to signify that the cycle will begin again. Although superficially Guy Fawkes night is linked to the attempt by Catholics to kill the king of Britain James I, the bonfires are in fact linked to an earlier festival Samhain (pronounced Soween), known colloquially as Halloween.

The name Halloween means the eve of all Hallows, which is All Saints Day (1st November). Halloween/Samhain traditionally represents the time when it is possible to communicate with the spirit world. The origin of pumpkin lamps is that they guide the spirits back to their home. It was also a time for bonfires, however with the growth of Christianity these were not encouraged. At the time of the death of Guy Fawkes the celebration of the festival was becoming more and more difficult because of the rise of Puritanism so it became the custom to describe it as the celebration of the defeat of the Catholic, Guy Fawkes. In the period of Puritan government in the mid 1600's this became a necessity. The puritans were well aware of the pagan origin of Christmas and in 1644 banned the celebration completely, even to the extent of prohibiting mass on the day. Although attempts continued to try and celebrate the fire festival at the end of October the church however was not deceived by the and created All Saints Day to attempt to nullify the effect of this festival. When the puritan period ended the repression of folk festivals gradually came to an end. As a result over the following 350 years the celebration of Halloween gradually became stronger and we therefore have two related festivals a few days apart.

Druids and the Summer Solstice

The situation with the summer solstice is more complex. Looking at this festival in more detail it was clear that this festival too has a folk tradition. This is reflected in Shakespeare's Midsummer Nights Dream where Puck and the other fairies come out on Midsummer Night and cause mischief. The summer solstice is also a time for well dressing. Wells are thought in pagan traditions to be spiritual places so this would appear to be the remnant of a pre Christian tradition. The most well known of all the celebrations however is the Druid celebration at Stonehenge, where Druids gather to view the sun rise. In order to unravel the origins of the summer solstice celebrations it is necessary to understand both the prehistoric period and developments of these traditions ion the early 18th century.

In the pre Roman period the periods are defined by the development of metallurgy. The three key periods are the New Stone Age (Neolithic), Bronze Age, and Iron Age The Neolithic is that period of the Stone Age following the adoption of agriculture.

In Britain this commenced in about 4200BC and continued to 2300 BC. The Bronze Age ran through to 500BC followed by the Iron Age. The Bronze Age occurred without external conquest, and although there was a significant amalgamation of kingdoms into a nation state at this time there was no external invasion. In contrast the Iron Age is integrally associated with the Celts. Although the Celts are often confused with the native British they were in fact blond haired and blue eyed Germanic Aryans who conquered Britain. Unlike bronze iron can be produced in large quantities to arm an entire tribe, which meant that the Celts, who were the masters of iron where able to take control of most of the British Isles. Caesar and other Roman writers define the Druids as the priestly caste of the Celts.

When they conquered Britain they did not populate it as the Europeans did when the conquered America, Instead they established an aristocracy as the Germans did when the conquered France in the World War Two. This can be seen by the fact that when the EEC did a survey of the genetic make up of the people of Britain they found that there was very little Celtic material with those whose grandparents were born in Britain having 95% of their genetic make up from the pre Celtic era.

The Romans report that the natives were treated poorly by the Druids. Additionally the archaeological record shows that slavery was introduced. This is indicated by the finding of slave rings used to chain those who had fallen into servitude. The spiritual traditions were also brutal. Caesar records that the Druids indulged in executions to satisfy their Gods. He records

"The Druids used figures of immense size whose limbs, woven out of twigs, they filled with living men and then they set them on fire so that the men died in a sheet of flame. Those who perished were generally common criminals but where there were no criminals they resorted to the execution of the innocent."

Such brutality is also indicative that the Celtic Druids were of a different ethnic group to the British that were the likely victims.

This is the origin of the concept of the Wicker Man. Ceaser also records

"They cut the entrails of living men and from them divined their future"

Clearly the Romans sought to justify their destruction of Celtic society, however there can be little doubt that the image of the Druids being kindly figures who merged with the native British is likely to be a romantic notion based on the traditions and behaviour of modern Druids who are widely viewed as an eccentric but none the less important part of modern British life. The key question when analysing these traditions is whether they had phased out these more barbaric practices or whether their traditions had been reconstructed in the modern era.

Druids

There are currently many Druid traditions, which join together under CBDO, the Council of British Druid Orders. This group has historically played a central role in liasing with English Heritage over the form of the summer solstice celebrations. The largest of the British Druid Orders is OBOD, the Order of Bards Ovates and Druids. This group operates publicly and has a noticeable presence. OBOD was a spin off in 1964 from the Ancient Order of Druids (AOD). This group has a long tradition going back many centuries. The AOD was formed on 22nd September 1717 by John Toland at a meeting in the Apple Tree pub in London. There are no reasonable grounds to believe that there was a true connection to the ancient Druids. The secret to understanding the Druids lies in the personality of William Stukeley who was the second head of the AOD. Stukeley was an early antiquarian and student of the Stonehenge monument. He also had access to the works of Caesar and other Roman writers which have many references to Druid traditions. It appears that he assumed that it was the Druids who had built Stonehenge. Seeing the sun rising over the heel stone on the summer solstice it appears that he assumed that it was the Druid tradition to gather at Stonehenge at that time. When carbon dating revealed that the monument was built 1800 years before the arrival of the Druids they continued to worship at the stones but dropped the claim to a Druidic origin. The Druids both ancient and modern also appear rather hierarchical and do not place a particular value in the circle, and it is clear to me that there is no direct connection between them and the builders of Stonehenge

Swords and Wiccans

The Druids are not the only spiritual path attending the summer solstice celebrations. The other major group in attendance are called Wiccans but they are highly secretive. They did however have a strong prescence on the internet particularly, in the late 1990's, at the web site alt.pagan. Wiccans at the site referr the book 'Wicca - the old religion in the new Millenium', as the best guide to the subject. This text provided a number of pieces of important information which were to guide me in the right direction in my search.

Wiccan Style Gathering

The first of these was that the circle was the sacred shape for their spiritual path. The second piece of information was that some elements of their tradition claimed a heritage back to the time of Stonehenge. The third was the fact that the sword was important in their belief structure and that those taking up the path had to forge their own sword either symbolically or in reality. They kept their secrecy because their tradition had been illegal for hundreds of years in the period up until 1951. This seemed to me to be far more likely to be connected to the original beliefs of the stone circle builders.

The book had a photograph of Stonehenge on it's cover. In the book it outlined the initiatory practices of Wicca. The author writes,

"After revealing the Three - fold law the initiator now promises to tell the initiate a further mystery. This is the mystery of the Legend of the Goddess. In the legend the initiate and others enact the descent of the goddess into the underworld, the land of death. Here she meets with God as the dark Lord of Death .... [in some traditions] a male initiate will enact a legend of the god. The male initiate is the encounterer rather than the encountered taking the role of the hero who descends to meet the queen of the underworld. In the welsh 'Mabignogion', King Arthur has to enter the underworld, Annwn to retrieve the of rebirth. Later stories in the Arthurian cycle describe the quest by King Arthur's knights for the mystical treasure of the Holy Grail"

Many Wiccans do claim that their traditions do date to the pre Iron Age era, a claim rarely made by Druids.

The Sword in the Stone

The next step in uncovering the legends was to look into the legends themselves, outside of their modern context. The particular focus was the sword which is at the heart of the legend. Arthur had been given the sword Excalibur by the lady of the lake, and had thrown the sword back into the lake shortly before going to the Isle of Avalon. This was not however the first sword in the legends, which was the sword that was pulled from the stone. I went to the original legend, Malory's Morte D'Arthur and read the text

"So in the greatest church in London .... all the estates were long all day in the church to pray. And when matins was done, there was seen in the churchyard against the high altar a great stone four square, like unto a marble stone, and in the midst thereof was like an anvil of steel a foot in height, and therein stuck a fair sword naked by the point, and letters were written in gold about the point which said this ' Whoso pulleth out this sword of this stone and anvil is rightways king born of all England' "

The key element is the phrase

"Whoso pulleth out this sword of this stone and anvil "

The anvil initially seems a particularly unnatural feature, as the pulling of the sword from the stone alone would be more beautiful. What has become widely accepted over recent years is that the pulling of the sword from the stone and anvil was in fact a metaphor for the making of a sword, in which stone ore is turned into a globule of metal and banged into shape on an anvil. The whole story was imbued with a magical air. Clearly the making of a sword would only have been magical the very first time that it was achieved. This is a clear indication that the legend dates from the point at the end of the Stone Age and the start of the Bronze Age. If the legends of Arthur do indeed date from the Bronze Age they would reflect the philosophy of that era and would reveal the ideology of the stone circle builders.

The reference in the legend to kingship being bequeathed on Arthur is to be related to the fact that the sword is a weapon, and the creation of it would lead to victory in battle. Towards the end of the Stone Age bronze was known from Europe. The British would have wished to the develop their own weaponry and an arms race would have ensued. The winner would very likely have been able to unite the various kingdoms and become the nations first king. In the current era metallurgy, particularly linked to Uranium and the atom bomb has led to victory in war, and a similar situation would have existed at the time shortly before the building of the bluestone circle at Stonehenge.

The site of this action is not recorded in the legends. There are however local traditions stating that it took place at Mitchells Fold in Shropshire. The site is a stone circle which has not been carbon dated but is thought to be from the early bronze age period. The reason why this site was chosen was that it was a significant manufacturing site for battle axes in the stone age. It is likely that the makers of this weaponry had a strong interest in making metal weaponry. Also it is on the route from Alderley Edge, an early site for copper mining, the key ingredient together with tin, and the Arthurian capital of Isca Silurum, or Caerleon. Tin itself was mined in north Cornwall, itself an area with stong Arthurian connections.

Mitchells Fold Stone Circle

Alderley Edge, a likely site for the first mined copper, is an important one for the Arthurian legend. The copper ore is so rich that it colours the ground and is known to have been mined in the bronze age from a shovel that was found at the site.

The shovel itself dates from 1750 BC, however there are also many stone implements found at the site indicating it to be a likely source of the first copper. The site also has many legends of Arthur and particularly Merlin. The site is reputed to be where Arthurs knights lie sleeping awaiting the countries hour of need, and where Merlin guides travellers to their location. As a result one of the largest pubs in the area has been named after Merlin.

Merlin is also the reputed builder of Stonehenge and reading the detail of the legend explains significant facts of the history of the site. I suggest that Merlin took copper ore from Alderley Edge and mixed it with tin from Cornwall to make the first metal sword at Mitchells Fold.

The concept of the sword in the stone being a metaphor for the making of the sword in the early Bronze Age has entered the mainstream. Francis Pryor, Chairman of the Council for British Archaeology, has publicly stated his support for the idea of the motif being based on Bronze Age sword making.

Geoffrey of Monmouth

I began to look in more detail at the origins of the Merlin-Stonehenge legend. As it turned out this legend is of great antiquity. It was recorded in 'The history of the Kings of Britain' produced in 1138 by Geoffrey of Monmouth. This book purports to be the true history of Britain from earliest times up until 600 AD, and claims to be based on a much older book which is no longer in existence. The section on Merlin's building of the stone circle stretches over several pages. It tells the story that a monument was required for soldiers who had fallen in a battle. Merlin was called to devise a monument that would provide a resting place for them. He knew of stones at Mount Killarus in

Ireland, and organised with Uther Pendragon, the father of Arthur to organise an army of 15,000 men to go to Ireland to seize the stones. The people of Ireland resisted but were defeated and the stones were taken away and erected on Salisbury Plain.

There has been significant speculation by commentators that there could be some kernel of truth in it. There were a number of problems. The first was the stones of Stonehenge did not come from Ireland. The stones were brought to the site over a number of centuries but the ones that were at the site in the early stages, called the Bluestones, had been clearly shown to be from the Preseli Mountains in Wales. The second problem was that the story was dated by Geoffrey to 500 AD when the stones had been put up in the distant pre Roman period. There were two elements of the tale which did make sense however. The first of these was that the stones had been brought by water. This was widely accepted by experts as being likely. David Souden in his book 'Stonehenge' writes

Stonehenge with smaller bluestones visible

"Water transport - either by sea around the southwestern peninsula of England or by river along the Bristol Avon and it's tributaries - probably enabled the bluestones to reach Stonehenge."

As it was only in 1923 that the Welsh origin of the bluestones was

proposed there was no way that Geoffrey of Monmouth could have known that the stones would have come by sea to the site.

There was a second piece of information from 'The History' that had a ring of truth to it. In the early phase of the Avebury monument a boy of 14 had been sacrificed, apparently to give strength to it. 'The History of the Kings of Britain' describe how Merlin was discovered. It is detailed how a tower collapsed while being built and how it was decided to sacrifice a young fatherless boy to appease the gods. The boy was to have his blood sprinkled on the foundations. In the 'History' Merlin was selected for this but he was able to show that there was a pool of water in the foundations and as a result he was spared and the tradition of ritual sacrifice was ended. There was no way that Geoffrey could have known of this tradition, and it provided a further indication that these legends did carry some element of truth.

There is an interesting connection between the Prescilly Mountains and his Merlin's home town. In the text Geoffrey writes

"They came to a town that was afterwards called Kaermerdin and they saw some lads playing by the town gate........a sudden quarrel broke out between the two lads whose names were Merlin and Dinabutius."

The text defines the location as follows

"Kaermerdin, later name of the town in which Merlin was discovered......; = Camarthen"

Camarthen was the nearest major settlement to the Preseli mountains from where the bluestones of Stonehenge were taken.

Even more surprising was that archeologists are now able to determine the quarry that was used to dig the stones and it is at the site of Bedd Arthur a megalithic site in the Prescilly mountains.

This indicates that there is some truth in the tale, but still the problem remains, how could Geoffrey of Monmouth got the location of the original place of the stones so wrong. The key to this lies in the geography of the Arthurian legends. There were a dozen mentions of Ireland in the 'Morte D'Arthur', the main Arthurian text. This seemed a surprisingly high number. In particular Merlins mother was said to have lived on the border with Ireland. Additionally Ireland had a border with Carmelide which is clearly in Britain. As I looked through the references to Ireland in the Arthurian legends it became clear that it was somewhere on the mainland, and that South West Wales, home to the Prescilly bluestones, looked a likely candidate. As it turned out the legends of Geoffrey of Monmouth only make sense if you view them in the geographic context of the Arthurian legends.

There seemed to be a strong case for Merlin having been the original inspiration for the making of metal in Britain. Objects like the hoover and the xerox that the individual or company that made an object often attached their name to it. In Britain we do not call swords Arthur's or Merlin's however in French meaning the definition of Merlin is as follows

"Merlin a metal axe such as that used to cut logs, especially very ancient type."

The Dating of the Legends

Since there is a widespread assumption by historians that King Arthur is post Roman it is necessary to look at the traditional dating of the legends to see if there was any evidence to see if there has been a deliberate misdating of the legend. The main version of the Arthurian legend is a text by Sir Thomas Malory that was published in 1485. The reason why this version is so popular is two fold, firstly the tale itself is beautifully written, and secondly it was the first version to be published in print form. Malory lived at the same time as Caxton the inventor of the printing press. As the first publisher he picked on all of the most famous texts in the English language and printed them. Malory had completed his version of the legend in 1471 and Caxton decided that his version would be the one that he would publish.

Malory's version, called 'Morte d'Arthur' or 'The death of Arthur' is a remarkable book, seven hundred pages in total but forming a cohesive whole it has dominated the collective understanding of the Arthurian tale. Film makers such as John Boorman who produced the classic modern film 'Excalibur' used this version as the basis for his work. In order to understand the basis of the legends it is essential to understand who Malory was and what was his motivation for producing such a major piece of work. Malory is a very interesting character with a clear motivation for writing up the legends, as he was a knight fighting in the wars of the roses. The wars of the roses were a long running feud between different elements of the British Aristocracy. The roots of the conflict went back to the Norman invasion of 1066. In essence Britain was divided into two factions, those who came over from Normandy, and those who originated in Britain. The situation was complicated by the fact that the demarcation lines were not clearly drawn between these two groups. The king, however was from the Norman side, and the British were trying to overthrow him and replace him with a British leader. Malory was captured, and as a result he was imprisoned in 1463. Despite a large number of general pardons he was never released and died in prison. This was because he was a political prisoner. Malory had been a member of parliament and was simply too dangerous to release. If freed he could have been a key element in a general uprising.

It was in prison that Malory wrote the 'Morte d'Arthur'. The reason for writing up the legends is that they were highly powerful politically as a source of inspiration for the British. Arthur was thought by the general population to have not died but to be sleeping awaiting the countries hour of need. Clearly a general uprising against a French speaking king would represent that and thus the Arthur figure therefore represented a threat to the state. Malory wrote up the legends in a way that made them readable for the general population. Malory did not however invent the legends. His book itself refers to other texts and a close analysis shows that it is largely based on the Vulgate cycle, a version of the legends written around 1200. The Vulgate cycle itself was written by Cistercian monks at Glastonbury Abbey and the circumstances of their writing of the legends provides the basis for them being placed in the post Roman era.

Arthur was important to the monks of Glastonbury was because in 1191 AD they had discovered the bones of Arthur and Gwynevere buried in the grounds of the abbey. The abbey itself had been established several hundred years before and was reputed to have been placed on the site of one the earliest churches to have been built in Britain. By the 1180's Britain was a Roman Catholic country and Glastonbury was the most powerful church in the land. In 1184 the abbey was burnt down in a fire and completely destroyed. Although the monks had great wealth based on tax free business interests such as the rental of farm land they did not have the resources to pay for the rebuilding of the abbey. There were only two ways to pay for the rebuilding, donations from pilgrims visiting the site or grants made by government through taxation. In this period pilgrims were relatively few, however the king Henry II was a devout Roman Catholic and he paid for the initial rebuilding work. In 1189, however, he died. The king who followed him was Richard I, known as Richard the Lionheart. Unlike Henry, Richard had no interest in paying for rebuilding work to the abbey. Funds were tight as Richard devoted all available resources to the fighting of crusades. As a result grants for the rebuilding work stopped and work on the abbey came to an end.

For two years work was suspended and the monks were left camped in the grounds. In 1191 however the abbot, having heard of a legend that Arthur was buried at Glastonbury, ordered for the grounds to be dug. Close to the abbey walls two bodies were found, those of a man and a woman, and they were declared to be the bones of King Arthur and Gwynevere. Publicity surrounding the finding of the supposed bones of Arthur led to a huge increase in the number of pilgrims visiting the abbey and the subsequent donations provided the funds necessary to restart the rebuilding of the abbey. Although the monks had found a way to cover the rebuilding costs they were faced with the fact that Arthur was now at the centre of their appeal to the general population. Arthur was, however, a particularly unchristian character, particularly in the light of the fact that his wife had a lifelong affair with his boldest knight Sir Lancelot. The main problem however was that King Arthur did not die but lay in wait of his countries hour of need. If that were the case his bones could not have ended up in the abbey. The monks needed a version of the legend in which he died and was buried in Glastonbury. They therefore wrote up a version of the legend in which Arthur died and was buried in Glastonbury and this became a major strand of the legend, although more traditional strands in which Arthur lived on in Avalon, the British version of the afterlife, continued to circulate.

The belief that King Arthur would be reincarnated is a strong indication that the origin of the legend originate in a pre Christian period, since this belief is incompatible with this tradition. Some also believed that King Arthurs spirit had been carried into a bird called a Chough, which was not supposed to be killed.

Since the Arthurian legend as written by the monks had been based on an earlier legend that was in a pre Roman context it is worth examining other texts left in a pre Roman setting. Fortunately one strand of the legend, entitled Perceforest, was not modified. The reason for this was that this version was hidden in a castle in at Hainault, along with a Crown. my personal view is that this version went underground at the time of the Norman conquest in 1066 well before the supposed discovery of Arthur's remains at Glastonbury. This is because the crown that accompanied it would have needed to have been hidden from the Normans. When the situation was stable 300 years later it was rediscovered, and was therefore unaffected by the Christianisation of other strands of the legends. In Perceforest the description of the round table is the same as that of a stone circle, the description is as follows

"He saw through great trees a well made round table of ancient construction, covered with flat stones. The knight walked across the arena and in through the door of the temple. He found the place in its simplicity the most holy that he had ever experienced. There was an altar towards the east where he mused for a while. Turning to the right he saw a rich throne. The sun, which was then setting, directed a single ray through the door of the temple onto the throne illuminating it brightly."

The temple is also described as being

"round, made of stone, and painted green inside without image or portraiture".

Another temple is described as follows

"In the middle of the flat clearing was a round table open to the sky, which had a vestibule at the east indicating an entrance"

The Perceforest variant of the legend of King Arthur represents something close to the original version of the legend.

Since the Vulgate cycle was several hundred pages I began to wonder how thorough the monks had been in their modification of the legends. The modernisation had taken place in a hurry at the turn of the 12th century. Given the scale of the operation the task could not have been thoroughly completed. If I looked deeper into the legends I felt sure that I would be able to find examples of how the legends had been modernised from a pre roman version.

I had seen in Perceforest that the Round Table was described as being related to the stone circles. I decided to look more deeply at Malory and the Vulgate cycle to see if the Round Table as described could have been modified from an earlier version in which there was a stone circle connection. The traditional view of the round table is that it was a large flat wooden table similar to a boardroom table. There remained a question mark over the possibility of whether a single table could have accommodated all the knights. In the legends the number of knights is described as one hundred and fifty. Malory writes,

"I shall give him the round table which King Arthur gave me. And when it is fully complete there is a hundred knights and fifty. And as for an hundred good knights I have myself, but I want fifty so many have been slain in my days."

One hundred and fifty is a huge number of people to sit around a table. If there were two feet between each knight it would have to have had a circumference of three hundred feet which seems highly unlikely for a single piece of furniture. The natural form for so many people to be in a circle would be to stand or sit on the floor. Additionally if they were to eat together the natural place would be outside. When I looked at the descriptions of the hall it did appear that it had the features of being in the open air. An example of a passage which can be easier understood in it's original context is the following from Perlesvaus,

"One Pentecost Arthur was at Cardeuil, and many knights had come to the court. The king was seated ready for the feast, and the day was fine and clear and the air was pure and fresh. Sagremour the Rash and Lucan the butler were serving the King, but just after the first course had been served a bolt fired from a crossbow suddenly hit the pillar in the hall before the king and so hard that every knight heard it as it struck."

The way that the day is described as clear and fresh indicates that the round table met outdoors. In post Roman times and earlier the size of windows was very small as there was no glass. As they were more like slits the state of the weather would have not been obvious to those in the hall. In the original version of the legends the description would have been of an open-air stone circle. When the legends were modified the reference to the weather was left in. A further example where an open air context makes more sense is the following passage from Morte D'Arthur where Malory writes,

"There came running in a white hart into the hall, and a white hound next to him, and thirty couples of black running hounds came after with a great cry. And the hart went about the round table, and as he went by the side boards the hound bit him on the buttock and pulled out a piece whereon the hart leapt a great leap and overthrew a knight that sat at the side board."

This description of sixty hounds running around the hall of the round table is much easier to understand in its original context of a stone circle where the dogs run into the circle and out again.

There is another passage where the modification is more explicit. For example in the Vulgate cycle the Round Table was described as follows,

"Now, good sir, in the meadow you saw that there was a hayrack, by which you should understand the round table. For even as the spaces of the hayrack are marked off by wooden bars, so there are pillars at the round table which separate the seats one from another. The meadow signifies humility and patience which spring ever vigorous and quick."

The description of pillars is similar that of a stone circle where there are pillars of stone. The reason for this reference to pillars is that they were in the original version of the legend and could not be removed without removing the sense of the dream to which the passage refers. As a result the monks have changed the pillars of the stone circle into the pillars of a Norman style hall.

The fact that the round table originally was a stone circle also explains another feature which is the fact that the round table is generally pictured as having a hole in the middle. This is related to the way that the knights are served with food which is specifically described in the tale. This is seen in the early photo below. There is also a gap which is to allow for the perilous seat at which no knight sits. Stone circles, including Stonehenge itself generally have a missing stone reflecting the same feature.

A number of stones have also been accidentally left in the story and appear awkwardly in the final version. In the tale of the Sangreal Malory writes,

"And at last he came to a stony cross which departed two ways in waste land; and by that cross was a stone that was of marble, but it was so dark that Sir Lancelot might not wit what it was. The Sir Lancelot looked beside him and saw an old chapel."

The reason for this stone is never explained. Another example is

"That evening after supper King Arthur went for a ride on the plain with the Archbishop, and they came to a high and solid rock. The king looked up at the rock."

It is noticeable that in both these cases the appearance of a stone has a spiritual connection. The likely explanation is that in their haste the monks did not remove these stones from the final version and they were related to pagan worship of stones in the original.

A good example of the true nature of the Round Table comes from Beroul's 12th Century text 'Tristan'. In it the author describes Perinis riding to the Round Table. There are six round tables in the UK, one is a known fake from the 14th Century. The others are all open air sites, predominantly henge like in construction. In Berouls text he refers to two of these locations, Caerleon and Stirling. The Caerleon site is a Roman amphitheatre, obviously postdating the Bronze Age, however another similar site Maumbury henge in Dorset was a henge converted into an amphitheatre. It is feasible that the same is true of Caerleon as the construction of Caerleon is much more developed and would have destroyed the henge. Sirling also has a round table which is a henge like monument near to Stirling castle. There is a stone slab outside the Palace of the Round Table which is reminiscent of stones at the edge of stone circles. Finally Beroul writes that the Round Table turns like the world. This implies that the Round Table was not originally wood in construction, but seen as an open air site turning as the world itself turns.

The full text is below

"Perenis went up the remaining steps, mounted his horse and rode away. He did not cease to spur his horse on until he reached Caerleon. He took great trouble in carrying out this errand and deserved a fine reward. He enquired for news of the king and found that he was at Stirling. Fair Yseuts' squire went along the road that lead in that direction. He asked a shepherd who was playing a reed pipe:
'Where is the King ?'
'Sir' said he 'He is seated on his throne. You will see the Round Table which turns like the world, his family sits around it'
We shall soon be there said Perinis. When he arrived at the palace he dismounted beside the stone slab outside and entered quickly."

The Calendar of the Legends

Having seen that the modification of the description of the round table had left clues to a pre Roman origin I continued my investigation by looking at the calendar of the legends. In particular I looked at the dates on which the major events in the legends took place, to see if there were remnants of a pre Roman calendar. I had determined from my earlier study that there were eight festivals in the pre Roman calendar. These were the solstices and equinoxes and the half way points in between. The dates of the eight festivals of the pre Roman calendar were

21st December

5th February

21st March

5th May

21st June

5th August

21st September

5th November

These festivals are integral to the Arthurian legends. Fortunately at the start of the legends where Arthur pulls the sword from the stone there are a large number of references to different dates in the calendar. This is because Arthur is required to pull the sword on many occasions to show that he is truly the only person who is able to do it. In the legends it is described as follows,

"So at Candlemas many more great lords came thither for to have won the sword, but there might none prevail. And right as Arthur did at Christmas he did at Candlemas, and pulled out the sword easily, whereof the barons were sore aggrieved , and put it off in delay until the high feast of Easter. And as Arthur did afore so he did at Easter. Yet there were some of the great lords that had indignation that Arthur should be king, and put it off in a delay until the feast of Pentecost and so anon [at Pentecost] was the coronation made. And there was he sworn unto his Lords and commoners to be a true king, to stand with true justice thenceforth the days of this life."

In another reference the same festivals are described,

"So after Christmas King Arthur let call unto him many knights and they arranged together to make a party and a great tournament and joust..And the cry was made that the day of the jousts should be besides Westminster on Candlemas day..And thus it passed from Candlemas until after Easter that the month of May was come, when every heart beginneth to blossom and to burgeon."

The calendar of the year is continued in the Arthurian text of Perlesvaus,

"He had letters sealed and sent abroad to all lands summoning Lords and knights to attend a court at Pennevoiseuse by the Welsh sea at the next festival of Saint John which is after Pentecost. He decided to hold it that day because Pentecost was too soon, and some of those who were attending would not be able to get there in time."

References to another festival Lammas appears in Malory as follows

"He lodged as a Lord in his own house, and set laws in his land as he liked best. And then at Lammas he went."

The final festival mentioned is all hallows

"The King let purvey for a great feast, and also he let cry both tournaments and jousts throughout his realm, and the day he appointed and set as allhallowmass."

The dates of the Arthurian calendar are as follows (in the case where the festivals move from year to year the earliest possible date is taken.)

25th December (Christmas)

6th February (Candlemas)

23rd March (Easter)

7th May (Pentecost)

24th June (St Johns Day)

1st August (Lammas)

1st November (All hallows)

There is a link between these dates and those of the pre Roman calendar below

21st December

5th February

21st March

5th May

21st June

5th August

21st September

5th November

The festivals of the Arthurian calendar all fall within 5 days of the festivals of the pre Roman calendar. The reason for this is that when the monks modified the dates of the legends they picked a Christian festival which was as close as possible to the original pre Roman one.

Once the legends are viewed in a pre Roman context other elements of the legends begin to make a lot more sense. An example of this is the connection between ships and silk in the legends. There are many passages in the legends where silk baring ships are described. These ships are always seen as very special. Some examples are as follows

"So at last they went to the ship all three, and found it richly hanged with a cloth of silk. So by that time it was dark night. Then suddenly there was about them a hundred torches set upon the ships boards and it gave great light. And there came twelve fair damsels and they saluted King Arthur on their knees."

"One night, as the king lay sleeping with the king beside him he awoke after a short slumber and could not get back to sleep. So he rose and donned a long grey gown, and leaving his chamber he climbed up to lean at the windows of the hall, which looked over the sea. He stayed there a long while gazing down at the seashore when suddenly he saw far away a light approaching over the sea like the beam of a candle; he wondered much what it could be. He stood ther watching until he made out what appeared to be a ship

..The craft was draped in the middle with the finest silken cloth, and the sail was lowered because the sea was so calm and still."

"And as he slept there came a voice that bade him to go to the sea..And upon the sea strand he found a ship that was covered all in heavy white silk..And as soon as he was entered the ship departed into the sea, and to his seeming it went fleeing; but it was soon dark that he might know no man."

The development of trade with silk bearing ships took place at the start of the Bronze Age. This would have made a great impact on people of that era and this is the reason for them featuring so prominently in the legends. From the evidence of the calendar, the nature of the stone circle and the connections of silk and ships the pre Roman origins of the Arthurian legends become clearer.

Interestingly characters and ideas from the Arthurian cycle do exist in the Greek and Roman records. The Greek record is particularly rich as they had an interest in foreign cultures. The Isle of Apples features, as do the Ladies of the Hesperides who are seen by some as the basis for the Nine Ladies of Morgan le Fey. Pomponius Mela writes in the first century,

"In the Brittanic Sea, opposite the coast of the Ossismi [of Brittany], the isle of Sena belongs to a Gaulish divinity and is famous for its oracle; whose priestesses, sanctified by their perpetual virginity, are reportedly nine in number. They called the priestesses the Galligende and think that it is because they have been endowed with unique powers; that they can stir up the seas by their magical charms; that they turn into whatever animals they want; that cure what is incurable among other peoples; that they know and predict the future - but that it is not revealed except to sea-voyagers, and only those travelling to consult them."

The Greeks also record legends of the British having a giant sleeping in a cave in an island. Some have seen this as being linked to legends of Arthur lying in a cave sleeping awaiting the countries hour of need.

Interestingly authors of fiction related to the legend often place the characters in the dress of a few hundred years earlier. Thus although the Arthur of the Twelfth Century is a Dark Age character, by the 20th century he is dressed as a character from the 15th Century with plate armour. Arthur always remains old but his dress changes to fit what is represented by this concept.

Arthur and the ancient monuments

The key to the dating of the Arthurian legends is to date the sites which have links to the Arthurian tradition. Throughout Britain there are a number of key monuments which have had connections with the Arthurian legends which come out of the folk and written memory. Some of these are very old. The following is attributed to Nennius with a date of approximately 800 - 825AD.

"There is another wonder in the country called Builth. There is a heap of stones there, and one of these stones placed on the top of the pile has the footprint of a dog on it. When he hunted Twrch Trwyth, Cafal (Cabal), the warrior Arthur's hound, impressed his footprint on the stone, and Arthur later brought together the pile of stones, under the stone in which was his dog's footprint, and it is called Carn Cafal (Carn Cabal). Men come and take the stone in their hands for the space of a day and a night, and on the morrow it is found upon the stone pile."

Arthur is not connected with all monuments from the pre Roman period, the sites of which are broadly equally stretched over a period of four thousand years following the development of farming in approximately 4200BC. If the monuments were named subsequently to the time they were built then the people who named the monuments would not have known when they were built. You can therefore assume that if all the monuments which carry the Arthurian name are carbon dated to exactly the same period then there was a King Arthur at the time that they originate from. Chance alone cannot reasonably be enough for all twenty or so pre Roman monuments that carry the Arthurian name to have been built within the time span of the life of one man. Although not all the sites have been carbon dated, it does assist with the calculation of the date of what are the two most important monuments, the stone circle at Stonehenge, reputed to have been built by Merlin, and Merlin's mound. This is a seventy five foot high burial mound four miles from Britain's largest stone circle at Avebury. If these monuments could be dated to the same period and if this was the first time that swords were made from a stone and anvil in Britain this would go a long way to showing that there was an Arthur living in Britain at that time.

The first task is to establish the date of the start of the Bronze Age in Britain. This is a complex task because the Bronze Age began earlier in other European societies. Metal was then imported from these countries making it difficult to determine the start of the British Bronze Age. However the growth in the amount of metal and the types of use which was made of it indicates the start of the Bronze Age in this country. The most common date assumed is 2300 BC. This is important in the study of the Arthurian legends because the pulling of the sword from the stone and anvil is a metaphor for the making of the first sword.

The next stage is to check whether this matched the date of the building of the bluestone circle at Stonehenge. When archaeologists looked at Stonehenge they removed the stones and took out animal remains from under them. From this they were able to determine with 95% certainty that the stones had been put in place between 2480 and 2140 BC or approximately 2300BC. This is the date needed to show a correlation. There is also a large mound four miles from Avebury called Merlin's Mound. The large mound at Silbury Hill had no explicit Arthurian connections however the way that it was built was identical to Merlin's mound, and it was widely stated by experts that the two were probably built at the same time. There has been no carbon dating of Merlins mound, however Silbury Hill has been carbon dated. When the mound was built the soil was dug from a pit to the side of the monument. Antler picks used in the digging broke and were left in the base of the pit. Two carbon dates were taken indicating a 99.75% probability that the it was built between 2047 BC and 2456 BC. The average of these two dates is approximately 2300 BC indicating that as the most likely date for Merlin's Mound. The carbon dating evidence therefore linked together the making of swords, Stonehenge, and Merlin's Mound.

Merlin's Mound is one of many Early Bronze Age sites linked to King Arthur. The henge called King Arthur's Round Table is near Carlisle, the site of one of King Arthur's three courts.

The Nine Ladies are also used for as the name of many stone circles. This is not related to the number of stones as they vary widely. One of the most interesting is the Early Bronze Age site on Stanton Moor pictured below. As well as the name it also has a King stone nearby.

Nine Ladies Stone Circle

Pushing along this line of argument also helps reveal the location of Camelot. Study of the legends shows that Camelot was somewhere on the border of Loegria. Since Lloeger is the Welsh name for England for those who live in South Wales it is fair to assume that Camelot is in Somerset. Additionally Camelot is described as being in the Kingdom of Camelerde which is the home of Gwynevere. Camelerde is generally thought of as covering the Somerset area.

Stanton Drew, the third most substantial circle in England, is a likely candidate for the location of Camelot as it was near to the border between South Wales and Lloegr. This is particularly interesting since the assumed date of it's construction was around 2300BC. Additionally Camelot was defined as being built from red stone, as is Stanton Drew.

Stanton Drew

In the legends the knights of the round table gather at Camelot and wait to see a marvel. One of the squires brings tidings to the king that a stone has appeared in the river with a sword stuck in it. When the knights go to the river they see that the stone is red. Since this redness plays no further part in the tale it is likely that it was an original feature of the original location of Camelot. It is described as follows in Malory.

"All the fellowship of the Round Table were come unto Camelot..In came a squire that said unto the King,

Sire I bring you marvellous tidings.

What be they said the King

Sir there is here beneath at the river a great stone which I saw float above the water, and therein I saw stuck a sword. Then the king said I will see that marvel. So all the knights went with him and when they came unto the river they found a sword floating, as it were of red marble, and therein stuck a fair sword."

Additionally the two sites of Avebury and Stanton Drew are joined by a long ditch called the Wansdyke. The word dyke and henge have the same meaning and in the Arthurian legend the feature of Wanhenche is described. Additionally there is a river at Stanton Drew as there is at Camelot.

A further issue to realise is that although Camelot is pronounced with a hard 't' this is not the original pronunciation. The legends state

"Camaalis was the pagan king who was the eponym [ie had the same original name] as Camelot"

The site name that is required is not that that has come into English after more than three thousand years of oral transmission, but Camaalis the original name. Three miles south of Stanton Drew is the village of Camerley. Alerted by a work colleague that Camerley was reputed to be site of Camelot I took a trip to the site. Local farm workers were able to point out the site of Camelot as being at a local beauty spot was at the end of the field over a fence. The site is a natural ampitheatre, a perfect place for the gathering of a group of knights. The actual site of Camelot is a triangular patch of ground now separated from other land by a fence. I crossed the fence and walked onto the site where I found stones buried in a circular formation, clearly the half-buried remains of a Bronze age stone circle. I had, at last, found Camelot.

The Grail Legends

After proposing the date for King Arthur a framework exists for understanding the Grail legends. In the public mind the grail is generally perceived as a cup of great importance used at the last supper.

Typical Grail Image

If we look at the two widely recognised source texts, the New Testament and the earliest grail legend we see a different story. In the New Testament the physical cup of the last supper is not particularly important, however in the earliest Grail legend, that of Chretien de Troyes, there is an important cup, made of gold, but no mention of the last supper. To get to the heart of the grail legend it is essential to understand how the two texts fused together in popular tradition.

The original biblical texts tend to the impression that the cup of the last supper was made of clay or wood. This fact is picked up on in modern culture where Indiana Jones finds a wooden grail. The physical cup itself is not at all important in biblical texts, whereas in the grail legend it is central. The New Testament cup is only important for what it contains, therefore the location of the original cup or its physical construct is not important in the texts - the impression given is that any cup would be appropriate as long as it was close to hand.

In John, the most romantic of the gospels and the one which might be expected to develop the story the last supper itself barely merits a mention. The entire event merits just 3 sentences.

"Now before the feast of the Passover, when Jesus knew that his hour was come that he should depart out of this world to the father, having loved his own which were in this world, he loved them unto the end. And supper being ended, the devil having now been put into the heart of Judas Iscariot, Simon's Son, to betray him. Jesus knowing that the Father had given all things into his hands and that he was come from God, and went to God, he riseth from supper"

In Mark, Matthew, and Luke, the same story developed fully is shared. The section that deals with the cup states,

"And he took the cup, and gave thanks, and gave it to them saying, Drink ye all of it; For this is my blood of the new testament which is shed for many for the remission of sins. But I say unto you, I will not drink henceforth of the fruit of the vine, until that day when I drink it anew with you in my Fathers kingdom. And when they had sung an hymn they went out into the Mount of Olives"

It is therefore the contents of the cup which are important to Christianity.

The cup appears to belong to the house and its construction is not significant enough to merit a mention. The physical cup is not mentioned again in the New Testament, or in the apocrophal gospels, and is barely mentioned in Christian literature until 1191. From 1191 onwards the Christian grail is mentioned in abundance, a situation which continues to this day. The events of 1191 are therefore critical to the development of the Christian grail.

When we look at the grail tradition we can see that originally the legends of King Arthur were kept alive by wandering Breton minstrels and in Cornish and Welsh traditions, and they were put into written form in the period 1000 - 1450AD. The older traditions make no mention of the common Christian connection, which begins with the development of the Vulgate cycle, written shortly after 1191. This work was produced by the monks of Glastonbury Abbey. After the burning down of the abbey in 1184 and the ceasing of reconstruction in 1191 the bones of Arthur and Gwynevere were 'discovered', and this led to an influx of pilgrims. Since the mainstream tradition was that Arthur had not died but lay sleeping awaiting the countries hour of need it was necessary for a version to be produced where King Arthur had died and had been buried at Glastonbury.

The inspiration for this came from a British writer Robert de Boron. At this time he produced an octosyllabic poem entitled 'Joseph d'Arimathae'. This is a version of the legend where the cup of the last supper is used to catch the blood of Christ on the Cross and is then brought to Britain. This became a commonly accepted story.

Recent investigation published in the major Arthurian Journal 'Arthuriana' in Winter 1999, as a text called 'Joseph of Arimathea, the Holy Grail and the Edessa Icon' has revealed that Robert de Boron did not make this up from scratch. De Boron's story is based in its critical elements on another pre existent tale from 8th century Georgia. In this version the central relic is not the cup of the last supper but the shroud, and it is this which catches the blood. De Boron simply replaced the word shroud with cup to create this central element. From this we can understand that it is highly unlikely that there was any last supper grail legend before the version that he created from his own imagination.

Don Scavone, its author writes, writes

"A fairly well known 8th c. MS from Georgia ('I Joseph')
considered by its editors to derive from a 5th c. original discusses
St. Philip and Joseph of Arimathea founding a church to the Virgin
at Lydda. Many will not be aware that another theme of this same
MS describes Joseph catching Jesus' blood dripping from the feet
in the NT burial cloth (the cloth already associated with Joseph in
the NT). It is the earliest recorded form of the blood-collection
theme and was imitated and embellished by other apocrypha from
both the Greek East and the Latin West. Robert de Boron used the
Georgian text almost verbum ad verbum, only altering the shroud
in the original to the Last Supper cup (=the Holy Grail)."

This is further emphasised by St. Boniface (circa 740) who stated
"Once our priests had chalices of wood and hearts of gold. Now
they have chalices of gold and hearts of wood."

This reflects a widespread informed current opinion as to the
nature of the artefact.

In contrast to this the Arthurian grail is definitely gold. Chretien
de Troyes describes it as follows.

"A maiden accompanying the two young men was carrying a grail
with here two hands; she was beautiful, noble, and richly attired.
After she had entered the hall carrying the grail the room was so
illuminated that the candles lost their brilliance like stars and the
moon when the sun rises. After her came another maiden carrying
a silver carving plate. The grail, which was introduced first was of
pure gold"

It is very educational to look at the nature of the grail in paintings.

In the early period, the 12th and 13th century the grail is picured a simple cup. This is seen from the wall painting of the Last Supper, Ickleton, Cambridgeshire, 1150-1200 and the Lords supper carving from Naumburg cathedral circa 1250, and Duccio di Buoninsegna's Last Supper 1308-1311. As the legend of Arthur's Grail spread the cup becomes gold, for example in Dirk Bouts The Last Supper from 1464, Huguet's Last Supper in 1470 and Ushakovs last supper from 1685.

Ushakov's Last Supper 1685

It seems likely from these texts and earlier investigations therefore that the grail was originally not an icon from the last supper, but a gold cup from the same date as the rest of the legends, ie dating from approximately 2250BC.

There are a number of sites claiming to be Arthur's final resting place. One of them is the Rillaton Barrow on Bodmin Moor in Cornwall. This site was found to be the site of a gold cup, one of only two discovered from Bronze Age Britain. In his book "Tintagel and the Arthurian Mythos" Paul Broadhurst, the leading expert on the Cornish Arthurian legends" tells the events of the opening of the grave.

"In 1818, miners looking for ballast started dismantling the nearby barrow known locally as King Arthur's Grave. Within a stone box like chamber they discovered a bronze dagger and a remarkable gold cup......This unique gold vessel continued its particular destiny: after some years of obscurity it was discovered at the centre of the British Monarchy. One version of the tale says that it was recognised by a visiting expert in antiques who happened to notice it being used as a shaving mug. Today it is on display in the British Museum, known as the Rillaton cup from the manor of Rillaton on whose land it was found."

This recognition of the site as being King Arthur's Grave may come from Leslie Grinsell who visited the site and spoke to some boys who lived nearby - they said they knew the barrow as 'King Arthur's Grave' and he published this in his 1936 text 'Ancient Burial Mounds of England'.

The British museum currently dates the cup at around 1600BC. This date was ascribed before carbon dating by Sir Arthur Evans who believed that its construction was inspired by the Mycenean civilisation. No attempt was made after this to date the barrow other than estimates that it is Early Bronze Age, whereas the date of 1600BC would be Middle Bronze Age. It is not definitively determined but a date of 1600BC does not seem to match the barrow. Additionally the shape of the cup is similar to clay cups from the Early rather than Middle Bronze Age.

In 2002 a second very similar cup was discovered near Sandwich in Kent, the traditional crossing point to the continent in the Arthurian legends. This was also dated by the British Museum as

1600 BC, simply based on it's similar appearance, but without any check as to whether the original date of the Rillaton Cup was correct. In this case carbon dating of the site in which it was found was carried out which revealed that the grave was an Early Bronze Age in use in around 2300BC, and not in the period around 1600BC. Rather than redating the cup archaeologists speculated that the cup had been placed in the grave later. The problem with this however was the similarity of the cup to large amounts of grooved ware at the site. Commentators have stated that there is a similarity between the Rillaton and Ringlemere cup to late Neolithic grooved ware, and it seems likely that both of them do date to the same dates as the barrows in which they were buried, i.e. 2300BC.

From descriptions in the legends it is clear that the cup and blade are a combination, and in the Rillaton barrow this combination was found. There are many other grave sites with clay cups and blades. Beakers predominate to the extent that this is actually called the Beaker culture, and these items appear to have a ritual significance because they are often found in graves. It seems that the Grail legends, with their emphasis on the cup and blade, are reflective of an actual tradition that existed in the Early Bronze Age and carried through into the medieval period.

THE MEANING OF THE GRAIL LEGENDS

Understanding the original context of the Arthurian and Grail legends allows us to get to the truth of the most complex issue of all, the meaning of the Grail legend. Understanding the grail legend is complicated by the fact that there are a number of different versions. In broad terms there is the Christian grail strand of Robert de Boron and the Vulgate cycle and secondly there is the original Grail legend of Chretien and Eschenbach. For the reasons explained in this text the Christianised traditions do not help in understanding the true meaning, it is the original versions, particularly the largest and most complete, Parzival that contains the clearest version.

Parzival is interesting because in the text he drops a number of hints that astronomy is at the heart of the grail mystery, links that can be seen when the grail does appear. There are also many references to black and white such as magpies, chessboards and the particoloured nature of Feirefiz, Parzivals half brother. Darrah in his book Paganism and Arthurian Romance, and a number of other writers have picked up on the significance of astronomical references, and suggested that these are represent the meaning of the grail tradition. The key astronomical reference is in chapter 9 where the hermit explains to Parzival the meaning and origins of the Grail legend.

He talks about the origins of the text writing

"There was a heathen named Flegetanis who was highly renowned for his aquirements..... this infidel Flegetanis was able to define for us the recession of each planet and its return, and how long it revolves in orbit before it stands at its mark again. All human kind are affected by the revolutions of the planets. With his own eyes Flegetanis saw - and he spoke of it reverentially - hidden secrets in the constellations. He declared that there was a thing called the Gral, whose name he read in the stars without more ado. A troop left it on earth and then rose high above the stars if their innocence drew them back again...... Those humans who are summoned to the grail are ever worthy. Thus did Flegetanis write on this theme."

Flegetanis is not a proper name, simply Arabic for an astronomer. He seems to have been able to expain to Kyot, Wolframs source, what the legend was about. There are many other references to astronomical/astrological features across the text, particularly at key points related to the grail itself. The story of the appearance of the grail itself is as follows

After succeeding in battle, and marrying, Parzival leaves his wife and comes across a King fishing on a lake near to a castle. The king invites him in and he is looked after the by the ladies and squires of the castle. He is then invited to a feast where there is a sick man. A procession enters and a number of ladies come through the door. Finally a woman carrying a brightly glowing stone enters. Parzival wonders what the purpose of it is but says nothing. Whilst the stone is present a feast is served which is created by power of the stone itself, but eventually the procession leaves and the feast ends. In the morning the castle is deserted and Parzival leaves. On the road leading from the castle he is berated by a lady who asks why he did not ask any questions. He is then informed that because he did not ask any questions the King will remain in agony and the land will be barren. Parzival is later told by a hermit the meaning of the grail, and the right question to ask - what ails you ? It is not until the final chapter that the events repeat themselves and he gets the chance to ask the question and heal the King.

A curious feature of the legend is the attention paid by Eschenbach to the number of ladies. He points out repeatedly that there are three groups, a group of 4, a group of 8, and a group of 12. Each of these groups are dressed differently. Finally the bright stone appears. The legend starts with the first group of four,

"At the far end of the palace a steel door was thrown open. Through it came a pair of noble maidens...The gown of the countess of Trebonic was of fine brown Scarlet....Then there came a duchess and her companion, carrying two trestles of ivory. All four inclined their heads, and then the two set up the trestles before their lord. They stood there as a group, one as lovely as the other, and gave him unstinting service. All four were dressed alike"

The group of eight is described as follows,

"But see four more pairs of ladies have not missed their cue.....These eight ladies were wearing robes of samite of Azgouc greener than grass, of ample cut for length and breadth, and held together at their middles by long narrow girdles of price. Each of these modest young ladies wore a dainty garland of flowers above her hair"

Finally the last group of twelve enters.

"The daughters of Count Iwan of Nonel and Jenis of Ryl had been taken many a mile to serve there, and now these two princely ladies were seen advancing in ravishing gowns !......Noble ladies who had been summoned to serve their went before the silver, four faultless maidens, and bore a light for it. And so all six came on..... Just look! you can see another six advancing in sumptuous gowns, half cloth of gold, half brocade of Nineveh (blue) These and the former six already mentioned were wearing their gowns cut parti wise of stuffs that had cost a fortune"

The reason for the importance of these numbers is never explained, however is central to archaeoastronmy and archaeoastrology. This is is the study of stone circles and of the building of stone circles. It is widely believed that megalithic sites, particularly Stonehenge, are the centre of the culture of the people who lived in 2300BC.

Stone circle sites are aligned with, and connected to the movement of the celestial sphere. Stonehenge is widely recognised to be built along the axis of the Summer solstice sunrise and the Winter solstice sunset. At 51 degrees north, and at no other point in the Northern hemisphere, the winter sunset and summer sunrise and other related alignments take place at diametrically opposite points. This means that a circle shape can be used to record astronomical events in a cleaner way than at many other sites.

The site of Stonehenge was built over a series of stages, however the alignments were similar throughout, albeit that different stones were used to create the alignments. The most prominent connection is the viewing of the summer solstice sunrise, which can be seen from any point along the axis by looking out of the circle to the Heel stone, which is a large stone outside the circle. What is not so well known, although widely recognised by specialists in the field, is that the other three points of the four quarters of the year also have alignments. These are created from the station stones that sit outside the circle and connect to other points also marked by the existence of stones at the time the original circle built with stones from the Preseli Mountains was erected.

The set up of the stones means that these alignments can both be seen from the axis which crosses the centre of the circle. They can both be seen from the same point due to the latitude of Stonehenge. The specific location of the site is important, because at other points of latitude this single axis model does not work. The fact that the Sun and Astronomy were important to the British is recorded in the Greek tradition by Diodorus who writes

"And there is also on the island both a magnificent sacred precinct of Apollo and a notable temple which is adorned with many votive offerings and is spherical in shape. Furthermore, a city is there which is sacred to this god, and the majority of its inhabitants are players on the cithara; and these continually play on this instrument in the temple and sing hymns of praise to the god, glorifying his deeds? They say also that the moon, as viewed from this island, appears to be but a little distance from the earth and to have upon it prominences, like those of the earth, which are visible to the eye. The account is also given that the god visits the island every nineteen years, the period in which the return of the stars to the same place in the heavens is accomplished, and for this reason the nineteen year period is called by the Greeks the "year of Meton." At the time of this appearance of the god he both plays on the cithara and dances continuously the night through from the vernal equinox until the rising of the Pleiades, expressing in this manner his delight in his successes. And the kings of this city and the supervisors of the sacred precinct are called Boreades, since they are descendants of Boreas, 'and the succession to these positions is always kept in their family."

The actual circle concerned is not specified, however it does provide a clear written record for stone circle solar and astronomical alignments. It also provides a date of the vernal or spring equinox as the date for the appearance of the God which is the key date in the Grail legend.

The key to the megalithic sites is the following the point of intersection of the sun across the horizon at sunrise. When you do this at Stonehenge you get a spread of 80 degrees with the spring equinox half way along. When you divide the period between the solstice and equinox into 3 periods, i.e. months, you get a series of intersections on the horizon. Due to the fact that the sun cuts further along the horizon, at an apparently faster rate as it gets to the equinox the split between the various months is not equal. The ratio between the stones in the arc to measure this intersectio is 4:8:12.

This ratio 4/24:8/24:12/24 underpins and links archaeastronomy and the grail legend.

In the legend after the ladies have entered the Princess enters, it is written as follows

"After this came the princess . Her face shed such refulgence that all imagined it was sunrise. "

This is a clear reference to the sunrise, so important at stone circle sites. He continues

"Upon a green achmardi she bore the consummation of hearts desire, its root and its blossoming - a thing called 'the Gral'. paradisal, transcending all earthly perfection !"

The same metaphor is seen in Chretien de Troyes who writes

"She was beautiful, gracious, splendidly garbed, and as she entered with the grail in he hands, there was such a brilliant light that the candles lost their brightness, just as the stars do when the moon or the sun rises. "

The fact that she enters after the 4, 8 and 12 sets of ladies implies that the time is the equinox.

In chapter 9 the hermit tells the meaning of the grail. Again he refers to the Equinox. Due to Christian dominance of the period it is viewed within its Christian construct, both of Good Friday and the nature of the world in the period before Christ, however it is clear that Wolfram is referring to pagan traditions as he is defining the pre Christian period.

"Today a Message alights on the Gral governing its highest virtue, for today is Good Friday, where one can infallibly see a dove wing its way down from Heaven. It brings a small wafer to the stone and leaves it there, then flies up to heaven again. Every good Friday, as I say, the dove brings it to the stone from which the stone recieves all that is good on earth of food and drink of paradisal excellence - I mean whatever the earth yields. The stone, furthermore, has to give them the flesh of all the wild things that live below the aether, whether they fly, run, or swim - such prebend does the Gral, thanks to its indwelling powers, bestow on the chivalric brotherhood......When Lucifer and the Trinity began to war with each other, those who did not take sides, noble worthy angels, had to descend to earth, to that stone which is ever incorruptible. I do not know whether God forgave them or dammed them in the end: if it was his due he took them back. Since that time the Stone has been in the care of those whom God appointed to it, and to whom he sent his angel. This, sir, is how matters stand regarding the grail."

This coming of the dove appears within the general context as a metaphor for the light of the sun coming to a megalithic stone on the equinox morning.

In May 2002 an excavation of an early Bronze Age grave took place at Amesbury, very close to Stonehenge. This grave came to be known as belonging to the Amesbury archer and dated to 2300 BC. When the grave was dug archaeologists discovered a cup and blade, the central physical features of the grail tradition.

When the connections between the numerology of the grail

procession and the sunrise is understood the large number of references to Astronomy and darkness and light in the grail legend make sense. The knowledge contained with the grail legends was at the heart of the Bronze Age society, and the key to its ritual. It is because this was the central ritual of this prehistoric period that such importance is attached to it - and is the secret as to why the Grail legend that contains it has such a grip on the western mind.